Original title:
Through the Twilight

Copyright © 2024 Creative Arts Management OÜ
All rights reserved.

Author: Elias Marchant
ISBN HARDBACK: 978-9916-90-058-1
ISBN PAPERBACK: 978-9916-90-059-8

A Waltz Beneath the Evening Stars

In twilight soft, we start to sway,
The stars above in bright array.
With gentle steps, we move as one,
In rhythms sweet, our hearts are spun.

The cool night air, a whispered song,
As shadows dance where we belong.
Each twirl ignites the moon's soft glow,
Together lost, we ebb and flow.

Refractions of Hidden Light

A prism's touch on morning dew,
Awakens colors bold and true.
The sun ascends, a golden blaze,
Through whispered clouds, it starts to graze.

In scattered beams, the secrets seep,
Where darkness stirs, in silence deep.
Each ray a tale, a story's start,
Of hidden dreams within the heart.

Threads of Daylight Breaking

As dawn ignites the sleepy haze,
New threads of light begin the day.
With every stitch, the world awakes,
A tapestry that sunlight makes.

Soft whispers chase the shadows near,
While nature sings, the path is clear.
Each golden strand, a promise bright,
In woven warmth, we find our light.

Moonscape Dreams

Upon the surface, silver shines,
In shadows deep, a dream defines.
The night unfolds a quiet grace,
A tranquil hush in space's embrace.

Through craters vast, our thoughts will roam,
In lunar lands, we find our home.
Each swirling star a whispered prayer,
In moonscape dreams, we breathe the air.

Radiance in the Quietness

In the hush of dawn's soft light,
Whispers of the world take flight.
Gentle rays break through the trees,
Cradled in a morning breeze.

Colors burst in hues so bright,
Painting shadows with delight.
Every leaf and petal glows,
As the day gracefully grows.

A Tapestry of Twilit Dreams

Threads of dusk begin to weave,
In the twilight, hearts believe.
Crimson clouds in indigo skies,
Hold the secrets, softly sighs.

Whispers in the gloaming air,
Stories hidden everywhere.
Dreams that dance on fading light,
Embrace the calm of coming night.

The Stillness Between Stars

In the void, a silence sings,
Echoes of the cosmos' wings.
Stars like lanterns far away,
Glimpse of dusk, a soft ballet.

Moments pause in endless space,
Time suspended, boundless grace.
Breath of night, a soothing balm,
In the dark, the heart is calm.

Glimmers of the Oncoming Night

As the sun begins to fade,
Silhouettes in shadows wade.
Fleeting moments, flickers bright,
Glimmers dancing with the night.

In the hush, the day departs,
Night unfolds with gentle arts.
Beneath the vast and velvet dome,
Silent whispers beckon home.

Harvesting the Evening's Breath

Golden fields sway in twilight's glow,
Gentle breezes in the shadows flow.
Crickets sing their evening song,
While the dusk lingers, soft and strong.

The sky blushes with hues of red,
As day shifts gently, the sun's bed.
Stars awaken, one by one,
A tranquil end to the day's run.

Where Day Meets Night

The horizon blurs in a soft embrace,
Where daylight fades, with gentle grace.
Colors dance in a fleeting sigh,
As day bids farewell and night draws nigh.

Silhouettes merge under the stars' glow,
Dreams awaken, whispers start to flow.
In this moment, time stands still,
As night wraps the world in its quilt.

The Last Kiss of Sunlight

A golden kiss upon the ground,
The sun dips low without a sound.
Shadows stretch and softly creep,
As nature prepares for a restful sleep.

The sky ignites in colors bright,
Signaling the end of light.
With every ray that softly fades,
Promises of night in serenades.

Whispers of the Waning Day

In the hush of twilight's glow,
Whispers tell what we cannot know.
The sun retreats, its warmth now wanes,
As the world wraps in gentle chains.

Stars begin their silent dance,
Inviting dreams with a fleeting glance.
Each breath brings a soothing sigh,
As the day bids a soft goodbye.

Last Light's Serenade

The sun dips low, in hues so bright,
Whispers of gold in fading light.
Shadows stretch across the land,
Nature's song, soft and bland.

As dusk descends, the day takes flight,
Stars emerge, twinkling in night.
A gentle breeze, a soft embrace,
In twilight's arms, we find our place.

Murmurs Beneath the Crescent Moon

Underneath a sliver of night,
The moon hangs low, casting light.
Whispers dance on the cool breeze,
Secrets shared among the trees.

In this calm and tranquil space,
Time slows down, a sacred grace.
Stars peek through, one by one,
Beneath the glow, we come undone.

Starlit Revelations

In the depth of night, dreams ignite,
Stars reveal what's hidden from sight.
Each twinkle tells a tale of old,
Messages of wonder, bold.

In this celestial tapestry,
Hearts connect, wild and free.
With every breath, the silence hums,
In starlit realms, eternity comes.

Heartbeat of the Hazy Hour

In the dim light of dusk's glow,
Time seems to wane, soft and slow.
The air is thick with dreams untold,
A heartbeat strong, yet quietly bold.

Moments linger, sweet and rare,
Echoes linger in the air.
As the world slips into a daze,
We cherish this last, hazy phase.

When Day Meets Night

As daylight fades, the shadows creep,
The sun dips low, the world in deep.
Whispers of twilight start to rise,
Painting colors across the skies.

Stars emerge in a velvet shroud,
The moon rises, serene and proud.
Nature sighs in gentle hush,
In this moment, hearts can rush.

The Edge of Dusk's Canvas

On the brink where day does cease,
Blending hues in quiet peace.
Brush strokes of orange, pink, and gray,
Mark the journey of the day.

Clouds drift softly, a painter's hand,
Sketching dreams upon the land.
As shadows lengthen, they entwine,
In the grasp of evening's design.

Secrets of the Waning Sun

Beneath the glow of a sun grown dim,
Lies a tale on the light's last whim.
Whispers shared in the fading light,
Secrets linger as day meets night.

The horizon swallows the golden rays,
Unveiling mysteries of closing days.
In this hush, the world holds tight,
To the magic of the coming night.

Dreams in the Dimness

In shadows deep, where silence dwells,
Lies the echo of olden spells.
Dreams awaken in gentle sighs,
Carried softly on the night skies.

With every flicker of the star,
They remind us just how close we are.
To the whispers of night, so still and bright,
Where dreams take flight in the dimness' light.

Serenade of the Setting Sun

The sky blushes in hues of gold,
As twilight whispers secrets untold.
Birds return to their quiet nests,
While the sun dips low, in its soft vests.

Gentle winds carry the day's last sigh,
Kissing the earth, where memories lie.
The horizon's edge melts into night,
A serenade to the fading light.

Where Shadows Gather

In the corners, whispers creep,
Where shadows gather, secrets seep.
Flickering lights dance on the wall,
Echoes of laughter, a haunting call.

Moonlight spills through the gnarled trees,
The world hushed, caught in a freeze.
Beneath the stars, the night holds sway,
Where shadows gather, dreams in play.

Beneath the Cloak of Evening

Beneath the cloak of evening's grace,
Stars emerge, each one a trace.
The world exhales, in stillness found,
While heartbeats echo, a soft sound.

Crickets sing their nightly tune,
As the silvery crescent cradles the moon.
In the quiet, stories unfold,
Beneath the cloak, both new and old.

Unraveling Daylight's Thread

The sun's retreat paints skies in fire,
Daylight's thread unwoven, desire.
Each moment lingers, a fleeting kiss,
As night drapes softly, a tranquil bliss.

Time unwinds in shadows' embrace,
Secrets hidden, a sacred space.
Underneath the stars, we find our way,
Unraveling daylight, welcoming gray.

Silhouettes of Breathless Beauty

In shadows cast by twilight glow,
Figures dance where whispers flow.
Each curve speaks of stories bold,
In silence, their grace unfolds.

Veils of night, adorned in lace,
Hold the secrets of their grace.
Every breath, a gentle sigh,
Underneath the velvet sky.

Fragrant blooms in muted light,
Paint the canvas of the night.
Their essence lingers in the air,
A reminder of beauty rare.

As dreams entwine with whispered fate,
These silhouettes, we celebrate.
In hushed tones, they sway and spin,
A timeless dance that draws us in.

Where Light Meets Enigma

In the dawn, a riddle wakes,
Casting shadows, the stillness breaks.
Eager whispers ride the breeze,
Mysteries wrap around the trees.

Flickering lights in hidden glades,
Guard the secrets the forest fades.
With every step, we seek the way,
Where the light and enigma play.

Reflections glimmer on the stream,
Hints of magic, like a dream.
Chasing echoes, chasing time,
In the rhythm, we find the rhyme.

Through the mist, the truth will show,
As shadows dance, and rivers flow.
In the heart of the unknown,
We discover, we find our home.

Glistening Eyes of the Nightfall

In the quiet, stars awake,
Glistening with every ache.
Eyes like mirrors, deep and wide,
Holding worlds that softly glide.

Each twinkle tells a tale untold,
Of dreams and fears, both brave and bold.
With every glance, the night conceals,
The truths that time only reveals.

Hushed whispers float on midnight air,
Eclipsed by wonder, faint and rare.
They beckon softly, like a song,
Inviting souls to join along.

With every heartbeat, shadows blend,
Life and longing gently mend.
In this realm where visions soar,
Glistening eyes unveil much more.

The Color of Lost Moments

In the palette of fading light,
Brushstrokes dance, both bold and slight.
Each hue whispers tales of yore,
Painting dreams we can't ignore.

Crimson sighs and sapphire tears,
Capture laughter, hold our fears.
Golden sunsets, memories sweet,
In every corner, life's heartbeat.

As time unravels, shades collide,
Fleeting moments we can't abide.
Yet in the tapestry we weave,
Beauty lingers, though we grieve.

Through the years, colors will fade,
But in our hearts, they won't evade.
The essence of what once has been,
Reminds us where we've always been.

Dance of the Gathering Night

Underneath the stars we twirl,
In shadows deep our dreams unfurl.
The whispers of the night surround,
In this sacred space we're found.

The moonlight drapes like silver lace,
Each heartbeat quickens in this place.
With every step, the world falls away,
In twilight's arms, we wish to stay.

The sky adorned with countless lights,
As we spin through endless nights.
In the rhythm of the dark we share,
A dance that lingers in the air.

So hold me close beneath the sky,
Where dreams awaken, time slips by.
In the magic of the gathering night,
We'll lose ourselves till morning light.

Reflections at Dusk's Edge

As day gives way to twilight's glow,
We gather thoughts, let memories flow.
The colors blend, a soft cascade,
In the hush where love won't fade.

Mirrored waters gleam with grace,
Captured moments, time's embrace.
In silence whispers tales untold,
A tapestry of dreams unrolled.

The sky ignites in hues of gold,
While secrets from the heart unfold.
With every sigh, a story shared,
In dusk's soft arms, we feel prepared.

Together we stand on evening's brink,
In the beauty of the moment, we sink.
As echoes fade and shadows blend,
In reflections, we find a friend.

The Horizon's Gentle Fade

In the distance, colors play,
As daylight bows, they drift away.
The sun dips low, a fiery dome,
Inviting the night to lead us home.

Clouds painted in shades of red,
Whispers of what the day has said.
With every breath, we capture light,
A fleeting moment takes its flight.

Glimmers of stars slowly ignite,
As darkness wraps the world so tight.
In this embrace, we find our place,
In the glow of dusk's tender grace.

So let us linger on this shore,
Where day meets night forevermore.
In the horizon's gentle fade,
Our hearts will bloom, our fears dismade.

Secrets in the Velvet Glow

In velvet nights where shadows sigh,
Soft whispers weave through the sky.
Secrets linger in the breeze,
Promises held beneath the trees.

Moonlight dances on the ground,
Each step echoes with a sound.
In this stillness, hearts align,
Tales of old in velvet shine.

The stars unearth their ancient rhyme,
As we indulge in love's sweet crime.
In the hush, our spirits fly,
Caught in magic beneath the sky.

So lean in closer, share your dreams,
In twilight's arms, nothing's as it seems.
With every glance, our secrets grow,
In the heart's embrace, beneath the glow.

Beauty in the Fading Gleam

The sun descends, a golden hue,
Soft whispers dance in twilight's view.
Petals close in a gentle sigh,
As day gives way to night's soft eye.

Stars awaken, a silver thread,
In dreams where light and shadows tread.
Nature's palette, rich and rare,
Holds beauty in the evening air.

Chasing the Colors of Dusk

With every stroke, the sky ignites,
Lavender whispers blend with sights.
Orange and pink, a tender embrace,
As daylight fades without a trace.

We chase the hues, forever bold,
In the tapestry of dusk retold.
Each fleeting moment, vivid and bright,
Carves memories in the fading light.

Shadows Stretching Wide

As dusk begins to weave its thread,
Long shadows dance where sunlight fled.
They stretch like dreams across the ground,
In twilight's grip, the night surrounds.

The world slows down, a gentle sigh,
While whispers of the night drift high.
In the silence, secrets behold,
Stories linger, waiting to unfold.

Lullabies of the Dimming Sky

The sky hums soft, a lullaby,
As twilight paints the world awry.
Stars shimmer gently, dreams take flight,
In the embrace of the coming night.

Nature's sleep, a sweet refrain,
Invites the heart to ease the strain.
With every breath, the dusk draws near,
And fills the soul with dreams sincere.

Emotions Wrapped in Evening Mist

Whispers linger in the air,
Secrets woven, hearts laid bare.
Shadows dance, a soft embrace,
In the stillness, we find grace.

Memories drift like autumn leaves,
Every moment, a heart that heaves.
Lost in time, our thoughts entwine,
Wrapped in mist, our souls align.

Flickering lights in twilight glow,
Like the dreams we long to know.
Softened edges, the world transforms,
In the quiet, the heart warms.

Together we chase the fading day,
Through the mist, we find our way.
Emotions pulse, the night unfolds,
In every sigh, a story told.

The Breath of Silver Night

Under stars, the night breathes deep,
A silent promise, secrets keep.
Moonlight spills on tranquil seas,
Whispers carried on the breeze.

Shadows stretch, the world is still,
Time suspended, hearts to fill.
In silver light, dreams softly play,
Entwined in night's serene ballet.

Each heartbeat syncs with twilight's song,
In this moment, we belong.
Mysteries wrapped in soft embrace,
Lost in night's transcendent grace.

As dawn approaches, shadows wane,
Yet in our hearts, the night remains.
Each memory, a silver thread,
Stitched in dreams, where love is spread.

The Beauty of Fading Horizons

Colors merge in twilight's glow,
Gold and crimson, whispers flow.
Horizons shift, the day retreats,
In this stillness, beauty greets.

Clouds brush lightly against the sky,
As the sun bids its soft goodbye.
Fading light, a gentle sigh,
Nature's canvas, a lullaby.

Each fading hue tells a tale,
Of love explored and winds that sail.
In the distance, shadows blend,
As light and darkness softly mend.

The beauty lies in what we lose,
In every choice, in every muse.
Horizons call, and hearts will yearn,
For beauty found in night's return.

A Haunting Prelude to Night

As daylight wanes, the silence grows,
An echo of what once was known.
Wind carries whispers, soft and light,
A haunting prelude to the night.

Ghostly figures slip through trees,
Carrying memories on the breeze.
With every rustle, shadows creep,
In twilight's hush, the world falls deep.

The moon awakens, pale and bright,
Casting dreams into the night.
Each breath a tale, a fleeting ghost,
In this darkness, we all are lost.

With every heartbeat, stories weave,
In whispered thoughts, we must believe.
A haunting dance, the night inspires,
As souls entwine in fading fires.

Beneath the Starlit Whisper

In the caress of night, we dream,
Soft starlight bathes all in gleam.
Whispers ride the gentle breeze,
Carrying thoughts through ancient trees.

Moonlight drapes on silent lakes,
Reflecting secrets that night wakes.
Each glimmer tells a story vast,
Of shadowed echoes from the past.

Crickets hum a lullaby sweet,
Nature's rhythm in soft heartbeat.
Underneath this boundless sky,
We search for truths, as time slips by.

Beneath the starlit whisper's glow,
We find the paths we long to know.
In the silence, hearts awake,
For every promise stars can make.

The Quiet Hour's Lament

As dusk descends and silence grows,
The quiet hour, it gently flows.
Time stands still, a breath held tight,
In whispers shared with fading light.

Memories hum a tender tune,
In shadows stretched beneath the moon.
Each moment lost, a fleeting ghost,
Silent echoes of what we boast.

The clock ticks slow, a sorrowed song,
In solitude, we feel so wrong.
Yet underneath the stillness sighs,
The hopes and dreams that never die.

In twilight's clutch, we seek and yearn,
For solace found in hearts that burn.
A soothing balm, this quiet space,
Where time, in whispers, finds its grace.

A Dance of Light and Dark

In the realm where shadows sweep,
Light and dark engage in keep.
A swirling waltz of joy and fear,
Each movement breathes a silent tear.

Stars ignite the velvet night,
As the moon takes center light.
Tangled thoughts like vines entwined,
In every heartbeat, fate defined.

Fleeting flickers of the dawn,
Bring life anew, the darkness gone.
Yet in the dusk, a subtle spark,
Remains in trysts of light and dark.

Through the day, we laugh and play,
In the night, we lose our way.
Yet in each dance, both realms await,
To guide us gently to our fate.

Fading Footsteps on the Path

Along the winding, dusky trail,
Footsteps echo, soft and pale.
With each step, memories fade,
Leaving traces where dreams once played.

The trees loom large, whispers near,
Songs of the lost we hold so dear.
With the wind, they sweep away,
Echoes of what once held sway.

Golden leaves beneath our stride,
Nature's canvas, our hearts confide.
Every turn, a story spun,
Of battles fought and victories won.

Yet as the path begins to wane,
We honor joy, we embrace pain.
For every journey, bittersweet,
Fading footsteps, our hearts repeat.

The Call of the Lingered Hour

In the hush of twilight's hold,
Whispers wrap the world in gold.
Shadows stretch, the day they cease,
Collecting dreams, they find their peace.

Time drifts softly, cradled sighs,
As stars awaken, fill the skies.
Moments linger, heartbeat's flow,
In this stillness, hearts will glow.

Echoes dance on evening's breath,
Life reflects in shades of death.
Each second sways, a tender tryst,
In the lingered hour's mist.

Softly fading, dusk does weave,
Magic tales, for those who believe.
The call of night brings sweet repose,
As time gently folds and slows.

Between Light and Remembering

In the dawn of memory's grace,
Flickers of light begin to chase.
Footsteps linger on the shore,
Each wave whispers, want for more.

Between the dark and morning's song,
Where cherished dreams and hopes belong.
Time's embrace, a gentle balm,
Filling hearts with timeless calm.

Reflections in a silver stream,
Night holds secrets, day a dream.
Moments scattered, yet they bind,
In the dance of what's designed.

Cascading rays of fading strife,
Painting shadows, strokes of life.
Between the light, a soft refrain,
Where all we love will meet again.

Escapade into Night's Embrace

With the moon, we softly glide,
Escaping where the dreams abide.
Stars like lanterns lead the way,
Guiding hearts where shadows play.

A night of whispers, tender thrill,
Chasing echoes, dreams to fill.
In darkness deep, we find our place,
Lost in night's warm, soft embrace.

Laughter lingers, joy does bloom,
In the stillness, dispelling gloom.
Holding tight beneath the sky,
We weave our tales, forever high.

Moments drip like velvet rain,
In this escapade, no refrain.
With every breath, a story starts,
Merging souls and beating hearts.

The Storyline of a Dusk Path

Along the path where shadows weave,
Nature whispers, inviting reprieve.
Brush of twilight paints the ground,
In the silence, peace is found.

Each step taken, tales unfold,
Stories written, dreams retold.
Underneath the evening glow,
Mysteries in the soft wind blow.

Leaves and branches sway in time,
Nature's rhythm, gentle rhyme.
Every twist and turn we trace,
Guides us deeper into grace.

On this dusk path, hearts align,
In every breath, a thread divine.
Where stories merge, and peace will stay,
Unraveling in dusk's ballet.

The Last Flicker of Daylight

The sun dips low, a golden sigh,
Clouds embrace, as colors die.
Whispers float on evening's breeze,
Nature bows with gentle ease.

Stars emerge, twinkling bright,
In the cloak of approaching night.
The world slows down, wrapped in peace,
As shadows stretch, and tensions cease.

Night's embrace, so soft and warm,
Hiding all the day's alarm.
In twilight's arms, we find our way,
As dreams await the close of day.

The last flicker, a fleeting glow,
Promising what the night will show.
In silence, every heart can sway,
To the rhythm of the fading day.

Beneath the Eclipse of Dreams

In the quiet, a whisper flows,
Underneath where moonlight glows.
Stars align, secrets untold,
Eclipsed thoughts, in silver fold.

Shadows dance on the soft ground,
Heartbeats echo, a whispered sound.
Journey forth through twilight's veil,
Where fantasy and truth prevail.

Silent wishes drift like mist,
In the depths of night's soft tryst.
Lost in dreams, we dare to roam,
Finding solace, a place called home.

Eclipsed in stillness, we unite,
Together in the depths of night.
Beneath this spell, our spirits soar,
In the dawn, we'll seek for more.

Veil of Dusk

Veil of dusk descending slow,
Painting skies in dusky glow.
Echoes linger from the day,
In soft hues where shadows play.

Crickets chirp a serenade,
As daylight's warmth begins to fade.
Whispers weave through trees so tall,
In the stillness, nightbirds call.

A gentle hush wraps evening near,
Every moment, crystal clear.
Embraced by twilight's tender kiss,
In this calm, we find our bliss.

Stars awaken, twinkling bright,
Guiding dreams into the night.
Under the veil where silence rests,
Our hearts find peace, our souls are blessed.

Whispering Shadows

Silhouettes beneath the trees,
Carried forth by gentle breeze.
Whispering shadows, tales of old,
Secrets spun as night unfolds.

Footsteps linger on the path,
Echoing a muted laugh.
Stars above, a watchful guide,
In their light, our fears collide.

Moonlight bathes the world in grace,
Softening the evening's face.
Boundless dreams taking flight,
With the whispers of the night.

Shadows dance and stories weave,
In their arms, we learn to believe.
Together under twilight's hue,
We find our strength, our spirits anew.

Lurking Blue Shadows

In the hush of twilight's call,
Shadows linger, eerily tall.
Whispers dance beneath the trees,
Softly swaying in the breeze.

Fingers reach from darkened nooks,
Drawing tales from ancient books.
Silhouettes with secrets hide,
In the night, where fears abide.

The moon peeks through a veil of gray,
Casting dreams that float away.
Blue shadows play on cobbled stones,
Keeping watch as silence roams.

In this world where shadows creep,
Only those with courage leap.
Through the dark, the heart must tread,
Lurking blue, where dreams are fed.

Paths Made of Dim Light

Faintly glowing, winding trails,
Guided by the quiet gales.
With each step, the night unfolds,
Stories lost in darkened molds.

Echoes whisper through the trees,
Carried softly on the breeze.
In the shadows, visions flare,
A tapestry of dreams laid bare.

While the stars hang low and bright,
Chasing paths made of dim light.
Guiding souls who dare to roam,
Finding solace far from home.

Embrace the dusk, let go of fear,
In the quiet, truth draws near.
Through each turn, the heart finds grace,
On these paths, a sacred space.

A Nocturnal Symphony

Moonlight bathes the sleeping earth,
A symphony of stars gives birth.
Crickets chirp a gentle tune,
Underneath a watchful moon.

Whispers rise with night's embrace,
Nature's pulse, a sacred place.
Rustling leaves, a soft refrain,
Echoes linger, sweet as rain.

In the dark, where dreams take flight,
Melodies dance in whispers bright.
Join the chorus of the night,
Lost in harmony's delight.

Every sigh, a note to play,
In this nocturnal ballet.
Follow notes where shadows lead,
In the symphony, we are freed.

The Fading Breath of Day

Golden hues begin to sway,
As the sun melts into gray.
Whispers echo through the sky,
As light bids the world goodbye.

Crimson clouds wrap round the night,
Painting dreams in soft twilight.
Moments whisper, time does sway,
In the fading breath of day.

Stars will shine, the dusk keeps time,
Nature's lullaby, a rhyme.
In the quiet, shadows play,
Holding close the light's decay.

With each blink, the sun retreats,
In the dark, the heart competes.
Finding solace, come what may,
In the fading breath of day.

A Palette of Dusky Hues

Whispers of twilight paint the sky,
Colors blend as the day bids goodbye.
Crimson embraces the fading light,
While indigo dances with the night.

Misty shadows fall on the ground,
In silence, the secrets of dusk abound.
Amber touches the edge of dreams,
Echoes of beauty in silent themes.

Soft brushstrokes of violet grace,
Every hue tells a timeless place.
Nature's canvas, a tranquil view,
In every moment, a palette anew.

With each sigh, the shadows expand,
Painting stories with a delicate hand.
In dusky hues, our hearts will find,
Echoes of love, forever entwined.

Shadows Speak Softly

In the dark, where quiet lives,
Shadows whisper where the heart gives.
Secrets linger on the cool breeze,
Comfort found amidst the trees.

Barefoot on a path of leaves,
Moonlight shimmers and deceives.
Every silhouette tells a tale,
Of dreams that flicker, frail and pale.

Voices in whispers, soft as sighs,
Murmurs of past in the starry skies.
Through the night, shadows respond,
In their depths, a memory bond.

Silence knows the stories we hold,
In the dark, our truths unfold.
Shadows speak, and hearts will hear,
The gentle echoes of those near.

The Fade into Enchantment

As twilight drapes its velvet sheen,
Worlds untold begin to glean.
Fading light and sparks ignite,
Dreams awaken in the night.

Time unravels in the soft glow,
Where enchantments start to flow.
Every whisper has a chance,
Inviting all into a dance.

Stars emerge, twinkling bright,
Guiding souls with gentle light.
In this moment, hearts align,
Finding solace, pure and fine.

Upon the edge of dusk we stand,
Held by magic, hand in hand.
In fading colors, dreams take flight,
A journey born from the night.

Secrets Beneath the Starlit Veil

Beneath the sky of endless chance,
Whispers weave in a cosmic dance.
Stars above hold tales so deep,
Secrets hidden, but never asleep.

A silver thread connects the souls,
In twilight's hush, the universe rolls.
Eternal night in its gentle embrace,
Keeps the wonders of time and space.

Each twinkling light, a wish upon,
Promises made as the light is drawn.
In the quiet, dreams interlace,
Under the starlit veil, we find our place.

With every breath, the secrets twine,
In the silence, the heart will shine.
Together we share this endless night,
Embracing mystery, love, and light.

The Afterglow of Dreams

In shadows, whispers softly play,
The thoughts of night, they softly sway.
A gaze upon the fading light,
As stars awaken, bright and white.

Each moment hangs like a sweet sigh,
Painting the darkening heavens high.
Within the dreams, our hearts take flight,
Chasing the echoes of the night.

A canvas drawn with fleeting grace,
Memories linger, time won't erase.
In twilight's arms, we gently blend,
The afterglow that will not end.

So close your eyes, let go of fear,
For in your dreams, the world is clear.
Beyond the dawn, the soul will roam,
To realms of peace, we find our home.

Melodies of the Hushing Night

Upon the breeze, a tune does weave,
Wrapped in the calm, we dare believe.
The world retreats, as whispers grow,
In melodies of the hushing glow.

Each note a star that softly shines,
Revealing secrets in tangled vines.
A serenade for those who hear,
The music of the night draws near.

The crickets sing, the owls respond,
In symphonies of the twilight bond.
Beneath the sky, our worries fade,
As night unfolds its serenade.

So let your heart sway to the beat,
In the embrace of night, so sweet.
With every sound, our spirits flow,
To dance within the lunar glow.

Sighs of a Dying Sun

The horizon bleeds in hues of red,
As daylight whispers its farewell thread.
With every breath, the shadows grow,
Cloaked in the sighs of the dying glow.

The warmth retreats, a soft caress,
While twilight weaves its dusky dress.
In silence deep, the stars ignite,
Awakening dreams to fill the night.

So fleeting is this golden hour,
A moment's bliss, a fading power.
And as we watch the day recede,
In hearts, the memories take heed.

For every sunset holds a chance,
To find the solace in its dance.
In every sigh, a story spun,
Reflections on the dying sun.

Strokes of Twilight's Hand

With gentle strokes, the day departs,
Painting the sky, igniting hearts.
In hues of blue and softest gray,
Twilight beckons, inviting play.

Each brush of dusk, a tender kiss,
A fleeting glimpse of boundless bliss.
As shadows stretch, the world transforms,
Embracing peace in calming swarms.

The stars arrive to join the show,
Their shimmering light begins to flow.
In twilight's grasp, all worries cease,
Resting within the hands of peace.

So let the night wrap you in dreams,
While starlit whispers stitch the seams.
In every breath, the night commands,
The quiet magic of twilight's hands.

A Canvas of Soft Darkness

The sky drapes in shades of deep blue,
Whispers of night begin to ensue.
Stars flicker like dreams, gently set,
A canvas of soft darkness, quiet and wet.

Moonbeams paint silver on the ground,
In the silence, sweet peace is found.
Crickets sing lullabies to the night,
A soothing embrace, soft and light.

Shadows dance under the tall pines,
Nature's palette in delicate lines.
The world slows down, breaths intertwine,
As darkness settles, hearts align.

In this embrace where worries cease,
The night wraps us in tranquil peace.
A canvas of soft darkness, we see,
Reflections of dreams, wild and free.

Nightfall's Tender Embrace

The sun dips low, in its final bow,
As nightfall whispers, 'I am here now.'
Stars emerge, a shimmering lace,
Wrapping the world in night's embrace.

Gentle breezes kiss the trees,
Floating softly like a warm tease.
Moonlight glimmers on the lake,
A soft touch that dreams awake.

In shadows deep, secrets hide,
Wandering thoughts no longer bide.
Birds settle down, the sky grows bare,
In nightfall's grip, we breathe the air.

Tender moments, lost in time,
The heart beats slow, to night's soft rhyme.
Wrapped in darkness, we find our space,
In nightfall's tender, warm embrace.

The Elusive Glow

In the stillness of a quiet eve,
Dreams awaken, inviting reprieve.
The stars twinkle in a velvet dome,
Their elusive glow feels like home.

Gentle reminders of a day gone by,
Soft sparks that shimmer in the sky.
Whispers of hope, in shadows cast,
A light that beckons, holding fast.

Dance of the fireflies, fragile and bright,
Guiding our souls through the velvet night.
Moments we cherish, fleeting yet bold,
In the fleeting warmth of their glow, we hold.

The secret of night, in silence flows,
The Elusive Glow, where magic grows.
With hearts wide open, we embrace the flight,
Chasing the dreams that sparkle in night.

Fading Echoes of Daylight

Sunset hues begin to blend,
The day's warm glow starts to bend.
Whispers of dusk, soft and low,
Fading echoes of daylight flow.

Golden rays dip beyond the hills,
As evening silence softly fills.
Colors soften, twilight sings,
Of hidden magic that night brings.

A world once bathed in brilliant light,
Now cradled in the arms of night.
Shadows stretch as time moves on,
Fading echoes, a sweet yawn.

In the quiet corners, dreams take flight,
Carried softly through the night.
Fading echoes tell our tale,
Of daylight's beauty, soft and frail.

Beyond the Last Rays

The sun dips low, a fiery glow,
Casting shadows that dance and flow.
Whispers of night begin to sing,
Embracing the calm that twilight brings.

Stars peek through the velvety blue,
Secrets held in the night anew.
Dreams take flight on silken wings,
Beyond the last rays, hope springs.

Canvas of the Dusk

Brushstrokes of orange and purple blend,
The day takes a bow, it starts to end.
Clouds adorned in a golden hue,
Nature's art, forever true.

Gentle winds carry the scent of pine,
In this moment, hearts align.
Silence whispers in the fading light,
A canvas of dusk, a pure delight.

A Ballet of Fading Hues

Colors dance upon the evening sky,
As daylight fades, they softly sigh.
Lavender and rose begin to blend,
Nature's palette, world's perfect end.

Each moment shifts with grace and flow,
A ballet where only dreamers go.
In the twilight, stories unfold,
A symphony of hues, bright and bold.

Lanterns in the Thickening Air

Glimmers flicker as dusk descends,
Lanterns glow, as daylight ends.
Each beacon a tale, softly spun,
Guiding the lost, bringing them home.

In the thickening air, memories rise,
Chasing shadows, beneath the skies.
Hope ignites like fireflies' gleam,
In this moment, we dare to dream.

Night's Tapestry Unfolding

In shadows deep, the whispers play,
The moonlight weaves a silver ray.
Stars twinkle softly, dreams take flight,
As night unveils its cloak of light.

A breath of calm in twilight's grace,
The velvet sky, a vast embrace.
Each moment lingers, time stands still,
As silence wraps the world in chill.

The owls converse in secret tones,
While crickets sing in hushed, low groans.
Beneath the veil, the secrets soar,
In night's embrace, we yearn for more.

With every breath, the darkness sighs,
While constellations dance in skies.
A tapestry, both bold and bright,
As night unfurls its endless light.

The Silence Before Stars

The dusk descends, the world holds breath,
As shadows creep, a hint of death.
The sky grows dark, a canvas bare,
Awaiting gems with tender care.

In quietude, the night prepares,
To dress the void with diamond flares.
The hush of space, a timeless lore,
Before the stars forevermore.

The heart beats slow, the moment's rare,
A silent promise fills the air.
Each twinkle waits, a wish unmade,
In stillness, hopes begin to fade.

As night unfolds, the stars ignite,
In shimmering silence, pure delight.
Each spark a story, tales untold,
In the night's embrace, the brave, the bold.

Tides of Indigo Time

The waves of night, a shushing sound,
Indigo whispers all around.
Time ebbs and flows, so soft, so slow,
In tranquil depths, where dreams do grow.

Each moment dances with the tide,
A quiet rhythm where thoughts reside.
Beneath the sky, in shades of blue,
The tides of time wash over you.

As stars reflect on liquid glass,
The night stretches forth, a velvet pass.
In every wave, a tale concealed,
In indigo depths, our hearts revealed.

The ocean breathes, a gentle sigh,
Underneath the expansive sky.
In every ripple, a dream takes flight,
Where time and tides unite in night.

When Colors Collide

In twilight's glow, the shades combine,
A canvas bursts with hues divine.
Colors clash in a vibrant dance,
Creating chaos, yet sweet chance.

The azure skies with orange streak,
In every blend, a voice to speak.
Fuchsia flares and emerald gleams,
When colors collide, they paint our dreams.

The sunset bleeds, a fierce embrace,
While shadows fill the empty space.
Each color sings, a bold refrain,
In every clash, a soft, sweet pain.

Unity grows in palette wide,
In chaos' heart, we dance and glide.
When colors converge, we start to see,
The beautiful art of harmony.

Serenade of the Evening Breeze

The stars ignite a velvet sky,
A whispering song as night draws nigh.
Soft winds dance through the trees,
Carrying secrets with gentle ease.

Moonlight spills on tranquil streams,
Lighting paths of silver dreams.
Nature hums its night refrain,
A melody born from whispered rain.

Crickets serenade the children of night,
As shadows waltz in the cloak of twilight.
Each note a promise, each breeze a sigh,
In the evening's arms, we gently lie.

Holding close the fleeting hour,
Touched by peace and silent power.
As stars bear witness to our trance,
The evening breeze invites romance.

The Quieting of the World

Softly falls the twilight haze,
In stillness, find the heart that stays.
The bustling day begins to fade,
In silence, a new peace is laid.

Whispers in the air take flight,
As shadows blend with waning light.
Each moment stretches like a sigh,
In the calm, we learn to fly.

The world outside grows hushed and dim,
While thoughts of hope rise on a whim.
Time slows down as stars appear,
In this quietude, we draw near.

Let the calm embrace your soul,
In the stillness, feel the whole.
Each heartbeat echoes soft and clear,
In the quieting, nothing to fear.

Memories in the Lengthening Shadows

As the sun dips low, shadows grow,
Whispers of time begin to flow.
Each silhouette holds a tale,
Of laughter bright and heartfelt pale.

With every stretch of fading light,
Nostalgia dances, pure and bright.
The day's sweet echoes softly fade,
In the twilight, memories are laid.

Footsteps linger on the path,
In the hush, we feel the aftermath.
Each moment cherished, time weaves tight,
In the shades of dusk, we find our light.

Let the shadows cradle your heart,
In their embrace, never depart.
For in the dusk, our stories blend,
In memories, we ride the wind.

The Gentle Whisper of Indigos

In hues of blue, the night awakes,
A gentle touch that twilight makes.
Indigo breezes, soft and sweet,
Wrap around us, a calm retreat.

Stars twinkle like scattered dreams,
Bathed in the glow of silver streams.
While darkness wraps the world in grace,
Each flicker draws a soft embrace.

Let the indigos dance in your heart,
As the night unfolds, we take part.
In this harmony, we shall find,
The gentle whispers of the mind.

Breath of the night, breathe deep and slow,
In every shadow, let your spirit flow.
For in the indigos, we learn to see,
The beauty of night, wild and free.

Shadows Stretching Softly

Beneath the trees, shadows play,
Whispering secrets of the day.
Softly stretching, they entwine,
In the twilight, they align.

Dancing lightly on the ground,
Nature's pulse, a gentle sound.
As daylight fades, they softly creep,
In their arms, the world will sleep.

Longing glances from the sky,
As the stars begin to shy.
Shadows hold the last warm light,
Cradling dreams of coming night.

Twilight's Gentle Kiss

Twilight comes with tender grace,
Caressing night's familiar face.
Stars peek out, one by one,
In the glow of setting sun.

Mellow hues of peach and gold,
In their warmth, the night unfolds.
Every whisper hushed and sweet,
Time slows down, hearts skip a beat.

Crickets sing their lullabies,
In the canvas of the skies.
Twilight's kiss, a soft embrace,
Wraps us in its peaceful space.

Hues of Evening's Breath

Colors blend as day retreats,
In the sky where silence meets.
Cobalt blues and fiery reds,
As the sun lays down its threads.

Evening's breath, a tender sigh,
Painting dreams that drift and fly.
Gentle waves of dusk arise,
Cradling night in soft reprise.

The world transforms, a canvas bright,
As day surrenders to the night.
Hues embrace the fading sun,
In this dance, we're all as one.

Lullabies of the Fading Day

Softly now, the daylight wanes,
Sung by winds through golden grains.
Lullabies from distant trees,
Whispered secrets on the breeze.

Every shadow gently cradles,
As daylight's glow slowly fades.
In this hush, the heart will sway,
To the songs of end of day.

Nestled in the darkened hues,
Softly treading, gentle muse.
Every note, a tender plea,
In the night, we will be free.

The Palette of Night's Arrival

The canvas darkens slowly, soft and deep,
Colors dance in shadows, secrets they keep.
Stars begin to shimmer, like whispers bright,
Embracing the horizon, painting the night.

The moon spills silver, a gentle embrace,
Caressing the earth with a tender grace.
Inky blues and purples blend with the dark,
Nature holds its breath, waiting for a spark.

Silhouettes of trees sway in the calm,
Nature's quiet symphony, soothing and warm.
A nightingale's song drifts softly ahead,
Guiding the lost where dreams dare to tread.

So linger a moment, let magic unfold,
In the palette of night, let stories be told.
With every glance upward, find peace in the view,
For night has a beauty that feels ever new.

Murmurs in the Half-Light

Soft whispers of twilight caress the cool air,
As shadows stretch gently, no need for a care.
Crickets join in chorus, a rhythmic delight,
Murmurs weave together in the soft half-light.

The world holds its breath, perched on the cusp,
Where day meets the night, with a tender lisp.
Fading hues of orange blend to deep grey,
Sewing the seams of dusk at the close of the day.

A breeze carries tales from far-off lands,
Rustling the leaves, as if nature understands.
The glow of the fireflies, twinkling like stars,
Guiding lost souls, removing their scars.

In this fleeting moment, all worries release,
Magic of transition, a canvas of peace.
Hold on to the whispers, let them take flight,
Dance in the echoes of the murmurs of night.

Lost in Lavender Hues

Lavender fields stretch under a wide, blue sky,
Petals whisper softly as breezes pass by.
Every bloom tells a story, fragrant and sweet,
In this vibrant maze, my heart finds its beat.

The sun dips low, painting shadows so fair,
Golden rays filter through, enhancing the air.
As twilight approaches, the colors ignite,
A canvas of dreams, every shade feels just right.

I wander through blossoms, with thoughts pure and clear,
Each step wrapped in comfort, like holding what's dear.
The world fades away, leaving only my heart,
In lavender hues, where my soul can restart.

With every deep breath, the essence I find,
A reminder of calm, a peace intertwined.
Here in this moment, life breathes soft and slow,
Lost in the lavender, where memories flow.

A Glimpse of the Veiled Sky

The sky dons a cloak of mystical veils,
Hints of stars peek through as twilight pales.
Clouds drift like whispers, secrets they share,
In a world painted gently, softened with care.

Every hue tells a story of day's gentle end,
As the sun fades away, darkness a friend.
The night wraps around like a sweet lullaby,
Cradling the earth in a comforting sigh.

A shimmer of silver where moonbeams take flight,
Guiding lost wanderers into the night.
Each twinkling star, a beacon from afar,
Inviting the dreamers to follow their star.

In this veiled expanse, where silence is found,
The heart stirs with wonder, joy unbound.
Embrace every moment, let your spirit fly,
For magic awakens in a veiled sky.

Fisherman's Tale After the Glow

Beneath the fading sun, he sails,
With nets of dreams and whispered tales.
The sea reflects a golden hue,
A world unknown, vast and true.

He casts his line, the ripples dance,
In hopes of fate or fleeting chance.
Each catch a story, each pause a sigh,
The night's embrace, the stars high.

Waves cradle secrets, lost and found,
In silence deep, the heart's resound.
With every trove from ocean's floor,
A bond with deep, forevermore.

As twilight whispers soft and low,
The fisherman smiles, for he will know,
That in the depths where shadows lay,
A tale begins in the fading day.

Soundtrack of the Silent Night

Moonlight dances on the ground,
In the stillness, no other sound.
A gentle breeze, the world serene,
Whispers secrets yet unseen.

Stars align in heavenly bliss,
Each twinkle is a stolen kiss.
Time suspends, as hearts unite,
In the soundtrack of the silent night.

Shadows play on ancient stone,
Echoes of dreams that feel like home.
The air is laced with magic's thread,
In moments where the past is wed.

In this hush, our hopes ignite,
Guided by the soft starlight.
With every breath, a feeling bright,
We find our peace in the silent night.

Timeless Watch of the Midnight Hour

The clock strikes twelve, a chime resounds,
In shadows deep, where mystery abounds.
With fleeting time, the moments blend,
A soft embrace, where dreams transcend.

Underneath the watchful moon,
Whispers linger, a hushed tune.
Dreamers tread on silver paths,
In the midnight hour, silence bathes.

Stars ignite in velvet skies,
Each one holding a million sighs.
Memories twirl in gentle grace,
In timeless stories, we find our place.

As hours pass, we hold them tight,
In the embrace of the soft twilight.
With every tick, the world devours,
The magic found in midnight hours.

Whispers of Dusk

Soft shadows creep along the ground,
As daylight fades without a sound.
The breeze carries secrets, sweet and low,
In the quiet hour where wonders grow.

Stars appear, a gentle spark,
In the canvas of night, they leave their mark.
Whispers of dusk in twilight's embrace,
A moment of magic, a sacred space.

Echoes at Sundown

The sun dips low, the sky ablaze,
Colors dance in a fleeting haze.
Echoes of laughter drift on the air,
As shadows stretch with a tender care.

Nature sighs in a lullaby,
While day kisses night, a sweet goodbye.
Whispers of memories, soft and bright,
Spun in the fabric of fading light.

Veil of Gloaming

Beneath the veil where night descends,
The day's bright laughter slowly bends.
In the gloaming, dreams begin to weave,
Through the threads of dusk, we softly cleave.

A hush rests gently on the land,
Nature's brushstrokes, soft and grand.
Veils of twilight drape the skies,
Painting hopes with muted sighs.

The Last Light's Embrace

In the silence of the evening's glow,
The last light bids the world hello.
With arms outstretched in a golden hue,
It whispers tenderly, 'I will miss you.'

The horizon blushes, a soft retreat,
As day and night in stillness meet.
Embrace the twilight, hold it tight,
For every ending brings new light.

Embrace of the Evening

Golden rays surrender slow,
Whispers of the breezes blow.
Stars awaken, softly shine,
Night embraces, truly divine.

Shadows dance on quiet ground,
Nature's peace, a soothing sound.
Moonlit paths that gently gleam,
In this moment, we dream.

Crickets sing their evening song,
As the world feels right, not wrong.
Time stands still, a sweet embrace,
Night's allure, a gentle grace.

Lament of the Fading Light

The sun dips low, a whispered sigh,
Colors bleed as daylight dies.
Fingers of dusk stretch and yawn,
Soon we'll greet the tender dawn.

Clouds wear hues of twilight's weep,
Memories linger, dark and deep.
Nature mourns the day now gone,
Silent echoes draw us on.

In the hush, a heartache stirs,
As the darkness softly blurs.
Yet in loss, a promise grows,
For in the night, new beauty flows.

Journey Beyond the Gloaming

Through the mist, our footsteps tread,
Following trails where shadows spread.
In the twilight, spirits call,
Inviting us to heed their thrall.

Whispers weave through ancient trees,
Carried softly on the breeze.
Each path taken, a story told,
In the fading light, brave and bold.

The horizon glows in twilight's grace,
As we seek that sacred space.
Guided by the stars above,
On this journey, we find love.

Echoes of the Dimming Day

Echoes linger, soft and sweet,
As the day and night do meet.
In the gloaming, silence sings,
Carrying whispers of hidden things.

Footfalls light on dewy grass,
Time seems still, as moments pass.
Memories weave, like threads of gold,
In the twilight, stories unfold.

With each star that comes alive,
Hope is kindled, dreams arrive.
In the dark, the heart will play,
To the tune of the dimming day.

Milton Keynes UK
Ingram Content Group UK Ltd.
UKHW022050111124
451035UK00014B/1033